A Guide for Us

D1537556

Romeo and Juliet

in the Classroom

Based on the novel written by William Shakespeare

This guide written by Mari Lu Robbins

Teacher Created Resources, Inc.
6421 Industry Way
Westminster, CA 92683
www.teachercreated.com

©1997 Teacher Created Resources, Inc.
Reprinted, 2006

Made in U.S.A.

ISBN 1-56790-135-1

Edited by
Walter Kelly, M.A.

Cover Art by
Wendy Chang

Table of Contents

Introduction

Really good literature never dies; it just gets better as it ages! This is just as true of a good play as it is of a good book. Over and over we can return to it for enjoyment, and each time we do, we can say, "Oh, I never read it that way before! How wonderful!"

In *Literature Units*, great care has been taken to select pieces of literature to which one can return again and again as we do to old friends.

Teachers who use this unit will find the following features to supplement their own valuable ideas.

- Sample lesson plans
- Pre-reading activities
- Biographical sketch and picture of the author
- Play summary
- Vocabulary lists and suggested vocabulary ideas
- Each act grouped for study with activities including these:

  —*quizzes*

  —*hands-on projects*

  —*cooperative learning activities*

  —*cross-curricular connections*

  —*extensions into the reader's life*

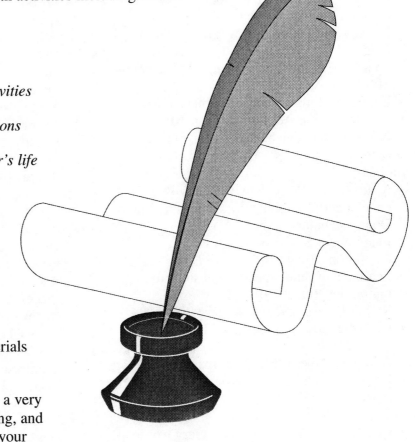

- Post-reading activities
- Book report ideas
- Research ideas
- Culminating activity
- Three different options for unit tests
- Bibliography of Related Materials
- Answer key

We are certain that this unit will be a very worthwhile addition to your planning, and we hope that as you use our ideas, your students will increase the circle of "old friends" to be found in good literature.

Sample Lesson Plan

Each of the lessons suggested below can take from one to several days to complete.

Lesson 1
- Introduce and complete some or all of the pre-reading activities found on page 5.
- Read "About the Author" with your students. (page 6)
- Read the play summary with your students. (page 7)
- Introduce the vocabulary list for Act I. (page 8)

Lesson 2
- Read Act I. As you read, place the vocabulary words in the context of the story and discuss their meanings. (page 8)
- Do a vocabulary activity. (page 9)
- Learn about Elizabethan clothing. (pages 11 and 12)
- Learn about the origins of English words. (page 13)
- Learn about how Shakespeare and the people of his time saw the world. (page 14)
- Begin Reading Response Journals. (page 16)
- Administer the Act I quiz. (page 10)
- Introduce the vocabulary list for Act II. (page 8)

Lesson 3
- Read Act II. Place the vocabulary words in context and discuss their meanings. (page 8)
- Do a vocabulary activity. (page 9)
- Learn about Shakespeare's use of oxymorons. (page 18)
- Learn about Shakespeare's allusions to mythology. (page 19)
- Retitle *Romeo and Juliet*. (page 20)
- Consider "love at first sight." Is it wise? (page 21)
- Administer the Act II Quiz. (page 17)
- Introduce vocabulary list for Act III. (page 8)

Lesson 4
- Read Act III. Place the vocabulary words in context and discuss their meanings. (page 8)
- Do a vocabulary activity. (page 9)
- Complete a *Romeo and Juliet* word search. (page 23)
- Read Shakespeare well. (page 24)
- Research Bloody Mary, Elizabeth I's half sister. (page 25)

- Write a chorus for Act III. (page 26)
- Administer the Act III quiz. (page 22)
- Introduce vocabulary list for Act IV. (page 8)

Lesson 5
- Read Act IV. Place the vocabulary words in context and discuss their meanings. (page 8)
- Do a vocabulary activity. (page 9)
- Experiment with air to see if it has weight and takes up space. (page 28)
- Survey superstitions. (page 29)
- Learn about alchemy and demonstrate the presence of oxygen in air. (page 30)
- Write a diary. (page 31)
- Administer the Act IV quiz. (page 27)
- Introduce vocabulary words for Act V. (page 8)

Lesson 6
- Read Act V. Place the vocabulary words in context and discuss their meanings. (page 8)
- Do a vocabulary activity. (page 9)
- Make a sundial. (page 33)
- Learn the differences between comedy and tragedy; rewrite the play's plot. (page 34)
- Learn about Ptolemaic Astronomy and display the solar system. (page 35)
- Write couplets. (page 37)
- Administer Act V quiz. (page 32)

Lesson 7
- Discuss any questions your students may have about the play. (page 38)
- Assign book report and research projects. (pages 39 and 40)
- Begin work on the culminating activity. (pages 41 and 42)

Lesson 8
- Administer unit tests 1, 2, and/or 3 (pages 43–45)
- Discuss the test answers and responses.
- Discuss the students' opinions and enjoyment of the play.
- Provide a list of related reading for the students. (page 46)

Lesson 9
- Celebrate the culminating activity, "Fish and Chips and Shakespeare." (pages 41 and 42)

4

Before the Play

When your students begin to read *Romeo and Juliet*, it may be the first time many of them will have come in contact with Shakespeare, and some of them may be a little anxious about what to expect. They may have heard that Shakespeare is hard to understand, that his plays are full of words they have never heard of, and that Shakespeare is only for "eggheads." Provide activities which will acquaint them with events of the time. Giving them ideas of how to approach Shakespeare enthusiastically can help them make the most of this new and rewarding experience. Here are some suggestions that may help your students to enjoy *Romeo and Juliet*.

❖ Predict what the story of the play might be by hearing the title.

❖ Read "About the Author," and discuss the fact that although Shakespeare had Queen Elizabeth as his patron, many of the playgoers who went to see his plays while he was alive and writing were common people who could not read or write. They were, however, very verbal and loved to play with the language. They would talk and eat and wander around the stage while the play was being performed, and they would jeer when they did not like something. Shakespeare had to work to keep their interest, so his plays are full of puns and figurative language which the Elizabethans loved, as well as sword play and excitement.

❖ Read about Shakespeare's world and what people of his day and age thought was correct behavior, and read the summary of the play. The play is about love at first sight; but to Shakespeare, love always led to marriage. *Romeo and Juliet* would never so much have kissed without being married, and if he had been caught, Romeo could have been killed for climbing into Juliet's room.

❖ As a class, see either a Shakespeare play or a film of one. The rhythm of the spoken language is very important when reading the plays, and some of the passages are written in poetry. Seeing a quality film or a live play can better help the students "get into" the rhythm of the play. *Romeo and Juliet* is a good play to start with, and you may consider seeing the Zefferelli film. *Romeo and Juliet* is a tragedy about love at first sight and about how misinformation can imperil a situation. This film version is an especially good choice for young people because its stars were only 15 and 17 years old at the time the film was made; therefore, it might be easier for today's students to relate to. There is a very brief nude scene in the film, so you may want to preview it before showing it to students and, of course, get your principal's approval for its use in the classroom. Following that, parental approval forms should be secured from each student who will be watching.

❖ Discuss the importance of reading *Romeo and Juliet* aloud, noting that it was written to be acted on the stage, not just read in the classroom.

❖ Discuss morality plays and the influence that they had on Shakespeare.

❖ Above all, enjoy the play.

About the Author

William Shakespeare was born into a well-to-do family. His father, John Shakespeare, was an established businessman in Stratford-upon-Avon who dealt in leather and glove-making and who rose in town importance from being chamberlain and alderman to high bailiff, much like being a mayor today. Although Shakespeare's mother, Mary Arden, came from a prominent Catholic family, it is not known whether he himself was ever a secret Catholic. He would not have been openly Catholic, for he lived during a time when Catholics were persecuted in England. Basic beliefs of the Roman Catholic Church and the early Church of England were very similar, however.

William Shakespeare was born in the house now known as The Birthplace. It was the custom to baptize a child three days after birth, and since church records at Holy Trinity Church in Stratford show his baptism to have been April 26, 1564, he is assumed to have been born April 23. The only records of births, marriages, and deaths were those kept by the church. He attended school in a half-timbered building which still stands in Stratford, and some think he taught there for a short time as well. He married Anne Hathaway when he was 18 and she was 26. They became the parents of three children—Susanna and, two years later, twins Judith and Hamnet.

No one knows for sure what Shakespeare did from 1585 to 1592, but by 1592 he was being mentioned as an "upstart crow" by a jealous rival dramatist in London. His first three plays were *Henry VI*, *Titus Andronicus*, and *The Comedy of Errors*. The theaters of London were closed between the years of 1592 to 1594 because of the bubonic plague, and during this time Shakespeare wrote his poem *Venus and Adonis* and began writing his sonnets.

When the plague was over in 1594, Shakespeare helped form the Lord Chamberlain's Men, which became London's premier acting company, in which he was both actor and playwright. Queen Elizabeth placed the company under her protection. This was important because religious groups known as Puritans were trying to shut down the theaters for being sinful and attracting the wrong sorts of people. The queen loved the theater and the arts, so Shakespeare's company was able to enjoy 14 productive years until her death in 1608. At that time, King James I continued royal patronage, and thereafter the company was known as The King's Men.

Shakespeare's plays and poetry were very popular, and from the beginning of his writing until his death in 1616 he wrote 37 plays, 154 sonnets, and other poetry. Around 1610 he left London for good and retired to his home in Stratford-upon-Avon, where he became an important member of the local gentry. In 1613 he collaborated with John Fletcher on *Henry VIII*, *The Two Noble Kinsmen*, and a play named *Cardenio*, which has since become lost. He died in Stratford-upon-Avon.

Romeo and Juliet

by William Shakespeare

(Oxford University Press, Inc., 1993)

(available in Canada, UK, and AUS from Oxford University Press)

The tragedy of *Romeo and Juliet* is the story of star-crossed lovers, two young people whose love and marriage are doomed as soon as they have begun. Their families, the Montagues and the Capulets, have maintained a blood feud in Verona, Italy, for many years, and members of each family have been killed by members of the other in a never-ending cycle of murder for revenge.

Romeo and Juliet fall in love at first sight when Romeo, a Montague, sneaks into a masked ball given by the Capulets and sees Juliet. With the help of Juliet's nurse and a sympathetic clergyman, they secretly marry, knowing that they do so at the risk of Romeo's death if they are discovered. When Romeo kills a Capulet in a duel, he is banished from Verona.

Meanwhile, Juliet's father, not knowing she is already married, promises her hand in marriage to County Paris. Juliet tries to change her father's mind, but he will not give in. The two young lovers separate in despair when Romeo is banished from Verona, and Juliet longs to be with him. Unknown to Romeo, Friar Lawrence gives Juliet a vial of a potion which will cause her to sleep as though dead. Her plan is to "die" and thereby escape the impossible marriage to County Paris and then go to be with Romeo after the "funeral."

Romeo, however, does not know of these well-laid plans, and when he discovers the seemingly dead body of his beloved Juliet, he kills himself. When Juliet awakens to find her lover dead by her side, she takes Romeo's knife and uses it to kill herself, this time for real.

Although *Romeo and Juliet* is one of the best loved of Shakespeare's plays, its story was a popular one long before this play was written, having been told before in Italian, French, and English. It is thought to be one of Shakespeare's earliest plays and was written while he was still almost a poet more than a playwright. It was based on an English poem by Arthur Brooke called *The Tragical History of Romeus and Juliet*, which was printed in 1562. The language of the play, however, is entirely that of Shakespeare.

Vocabulary Lists

Act I

chorus	mutiny	colliers	common
importuned	grievance	shrift	purge
discreet	forsworn	bound	reverence
joiner	grub	breach	portentous
vain	expire	forfeit	solemnity
semblance	choler	saucy	scathe

Act II

bewitch	conjure	consort	wanting
coy	chaste	frivolous	unadvised
attend	intercession	entreat	roe
conceive	despicable	convoy	prate
feign	jaunt	circumstance	wanton
confound	gossamer	lour	brine

Act III

doublet	livery	devise	appertain
bandy	villain	valor	untimely
truce	cockatrice	naught	dissemble
naught	beguile	affliction	doom
vestal	unseemly	digress	commend
fickle	procure	wreak	minion

Act IV

haste	pensive	prorogue	execution
charnel	reek	supple	abate
peevish	attire	mandrake	aqua vitae
rosemary	ordain	dirge	sullen
amend	minstrel	redress	tarry
bier	minister	behoove	cunning

Act V

post-horse	import	apothecary	cull
mortal	ducat	oppression	pestilence
aloof	detest	conduct	lament
restorative	impeach	perforce	privy
desperate	outrage	circumstance	ensign
pilot	wrench	muffle	dear

8

Vocabulary Activities

Romeo and Juliet contains many words which will be new to the students, some of which have obscure meanings because they are no longer used. Learning the words listed in the vocabulary lists, however, should help the students get a very good understanding of the play. If the play is studied orally, even a few unfamiliar words should not get in the way of student comprehension.

Have students keep a vocabulary list of the words they do not understand. Using the words in a variety of activities appropriate to the study of the play will help them remember and understand the words. Try some of the suggestions below for the listed words.

- **Illustrate a dictionary.** The Elizabethan Age during which Shakespeare wrote and acted followed close behind the first English printing press of William Caxton. Until that time, most books had been laboriously printed by hand and were often lavishly illustrated. Artistic students might enjoy making an illustrated dictionary of their own. Early dictionaries were printed with bright colors and a lot of gold. You might include in your dictionary only words which have their origins in French or in German.

- **Compile a glossary of words used in drama.** As with any specialized area, dramatic works contain a number of words specific to that area. Sometimes words used specifically in one field are known as *jargon*. What would these words be in drama?

- **Use the words to write a one-act play.** Write a one-act play or skit using as many of the vocabulary words as you can. The play or skit can be serious or silly, as you wish. Will your play be a comedy or tragedy?

- **Compose a soliloquy.** A soliloquy is a speech said by a character in which he or she speaks as though no one else is there. It is a way for the character to allow the audience to hear his or her thoughts. Imagine yourself to be one of the characters in *Romeo and Juliet*. Using several of the vocabulary words, compose a soliloquy which tells how that character feels at a given point in the play. Present your soliloquy to the class.

- **Invent an animal.** Invent an animal named with one of the vocabulary words. Draw a picture of your animal, list its favorite foods, its life habits, and describe its habitat.

- **Put Romeo and Juliet in a time machine.** Imagine that you are either Romeo or Juliet and you have been transported through time to the city where you now live. Write a description of your school, your home, and your street as it would be seen through that character's eyes.

Quiz Time

1. On the back of this paper, list three important events in Act I.

2. Who describes the setting of *Romeo and Juliet* to the audience?

   _____

   _____

3. Where does *Romeo and Juliet* take place?

   _____

   _____

4. Name the two families who maintain a blood feud against each other.

   _____

   _____

5. What does Capulet tell Paris to do about Juliet?

   _____

   _____

   _____

6. How are Mercutio and Juliet's nurse alike?

   _____

   _____

   _____

7. Describe in your own words the first meeting of Romeo and Juliet.

   _____

   _____

   _____

8. How does Romeo change after he falls in love with Juliet?

   _____

   _____

9. What does Tybalt want to do when he spies Romeo at the ball, and how is he prevented from doing it?

   _____

   _____

   _____

10. On the back of this page, tell how you think Romeo and Juliet's parents will react if they learn the two have fallen in love. Tell your reasons for having this opinion, and whether or not you think either of them can, or will, do anything to change their parents' minds.

Attend a Masquerade

Romeo and Juliet meet at a masquerade ball. This was a favorite kind of party for Elizabethans. They loved to dress up and pretend to be someone other than who they were, and they loved to wear masks in order to watch other people without being recognized themselves. Many people still enjoy masquerade parties, especially on Halloween or New Year's Eve. Look at the pictures on the next page to see how men and women commonly dressed in Shakespeare's England. Children's clothing was identical to that of adults, just smaller.

Elizabethan clothing was much different from the clothing we wear today. For one thing, sleeves were separate from the rest of the upper garments. For another, women's clothing was similar to men's in that both men and women wore garments which accentuated broad shoulders and narrow waists.

English winters can be cold, and a drafty house uncomfortable. The interiors of houses had only fireplaces for warmth, so men, and often women as well, wore hats inside. And men wore hose. Trousers and pockets had not yet been invented.

Activity

Imagine you are going to a masquerade ball where you are to wear only Elizabethan-styled clothing. Do one or more of the following:

1. Write a complete description of the Elizabethan costume you will wear. Describe your costume in terms of colors and fabrics, and include any accessories such as jewelry, swords, buckles, etc., that you will wear.

2. Draw a picture of yourself in your costume. Color it with the colors you intend to wear and then describe the fabrics and texture.

3. Make your Elizabethan costume. With this activity, you need to be aware that men's doublets and the upper parts of the hose which cover the thighs were stuffed with horsehair, wool, or rags. Women's sleeves were also stuffed, and both men's and women's sleeves were tied at the wrists. Ruffs at the neck were stiffly starched. Both men and women wore cloaks for warmth and to protect their clothing, which was seldom washed. Washing machines, dryers, and dry cleaning had not yet been invented. In fact, closets in which to keep the clothing had not been invented, either! Model or display your costume for the rest of the class.

Attend a Masquerade *(cont.)*

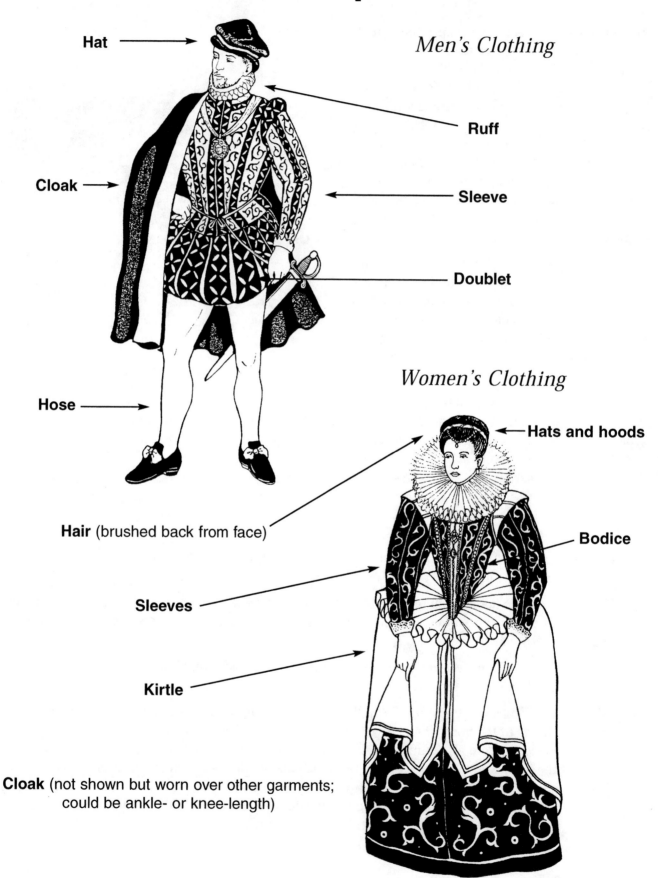

Men's Clothing

Hat

Ruff

Cloak

Sleeve

Doublet

Hose

Women's Clothing

Hats and hoods

Hair (brushed back from face)

Bodice

Sleeves

Kirtle

Cloak (not shown but worn over other garments;
could be ankle- or knee-length)

Update Your Dictionary

"The English language is the sea which receives tributaries from every region under heaven."

—Ralph Waldo Emerson

Have you ever wondered why there are so many inconsistencies in the English language? In many languages, Spanish for example, each letter has only one sound; so when you encounter that letter in a word, you know how it is spoken. In English, on the contrary, you sometimes can't tell by looking at a word how it is going to be pronounced. This is because the English language has developed over thousands of years from many languages to the one we now know.

English is thought to have begun about 8,000 years ago near the Black Sea in Europe as part of the Indo-European family of languages. When the Romans invaded the British Isles, they contributed Latin words to the language as it was spoken then. Successive invasions contributed parts of other languages. The Angles, Saxons, and Jutes gave us Germanic word roots (the core English vocabulary) in the 5th and 6th centuries. The Norman invasion in 1066 gave us French roots.

If you traveled in time back 600 years, you would have a difficult time understanding the old form of English spoken then because it still retained much of the pronunciation of the original Latin, Germanic, and French roots. The English language continues to grow, primarily through the combination of older words into new ones and by the addition of scientific terms and non-English words. Slang words are often old words used in new ways which gradually become part of the common tongue. Many words have more than one meaning.

Because of all these factors, English is an incredibly rich and diverse language. William Shakespeare used over 29,000 words in his plays and poetry! That is 23,000 more than were used in the King James version of the Bible, translated during the reign of King James I of England, Shakespeare's patron after the death of Queen Elizabeth I. Today, English is used by at least 75 million people (perhaps a billion, according to some estimates), only half of whom speak it as a mother tongue. Here at the close of the twentieth century, English is the most widely spoken of any language that has ever been. One might say it has become the premier language of the planet, fast becoming the first truly global language.

Activity

A good dictionary will supply you with the origins of English words like the word "gang," shown here:

gang (gang), *ganged, ganging.* Chiefly Scot. *to go.* (bef. 900; ME: OE *gangan, gongan*)

This entry shows us the word *gang* was originally a Scottish word meaning *to go*, that it has been part of English since before 900 A.D., and was part of Middle English (ME) and Old English (OE). One modern meaning might be "to go together."

In groups of four or five, compile a dictionary of at least 20 words which you have taken from *Romeo and Juliet*. Show the derivations of each of these words as has been done for you above.

How Shakespeare Saw the World

The world of William Shakespeare was much smaller than the one in which we live today. The parameters of how a person could behave and what a person could believe in were limited. Religious and personal freedoms which we consider so important today were unknown to the people of Shakespeare's England. To fully appreciate a play by Shakespeare, it is helpful to understand how he and his fellow citizens viewed the world.

They saw the world as a huge morality play written, staged, and directed by God. In this play there were only good and evil, with nothing in between. Everything happened so there would be a balance between good and evil. If the king or queen was cruel and tyrannical, or if a family was struck by a devastating illness or misfortune, it was a sign that God was punishing them. Going against what was taught to be God's will would certainly lead to severe punishment in life and hell after death. There was no mistaking right and wrong. They were taught in the lessons of the church.

God was ruler of everything and everyone. Events occurred according to what he wanted. There were no accidents. The church and its leaders were representatives of God on earth, and the king was king because God intended him to be. Everyone else existed at lower social levels, with noblemen and churchmen above the common people. Queen Elizabeth held the authority which otherwise would have gone to a king.

Children had no rights except those allowed by their parents. Teenagers had to obey every wish of their parents until they married, and marriage was usually arranged by the parents with little concern for the child's desires. Children married young, often by 14 or 15. A wife was obliged to obey her husband, just as she had obeyed her father. A father had the God-given right to force his daughter to marry a man she did not love. If she refused, he could send her to a convent (or perhaps worse) for the rest of her life, and she could do nothing about it.

The earth was the center of the universe with God and church in charge. God had made the king the center of the country. A father was the center of his home, and the "king" of his own castle-home. Everyone was obliged to obey this order. There were severe social and political penalties for anyone daring to go against it.

Activity

Complete the Venn diagram on the next page as directed:

- In Section **A** list values and beliefs which were held by the people of Shakespeare's England but which are not held by your people.

- In Section **C** list values and beliefs which your people hold today but which were not held by the people of Shakespeare's England.

- In Section **B** list characteristic values and beliefs which both you and the people of Shakespeare's time hold. Compare your diagram to those of your classmates and discuss the similarities and differences.

How Shakespeare Saw the World *(cont.)*

Venn Diagram

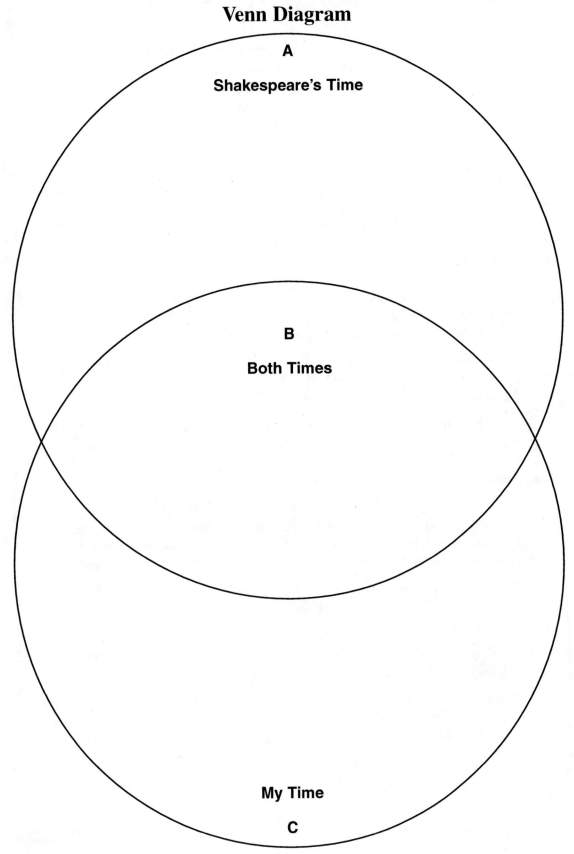

A

Shakespeare's Time

B

Both Times

My Time

C

Reading Response Journals

What better gifts can a teacher give students than a love for the spoken and written word and an ability to relate personally to literature? The English language is rich and alive because it continually changes and grows with frequent use. The more that students use the language by hearing it, speaking it, and writing it, the better they will be able to fully enjoy and cherish it.

Learning the skills of comprehending and using English in a multitude of ways will prepare your students for a modern world which is becoming more and more dependent on communicating well. Good comprehension comes from developing a personal relationship with the spoken and written word. Good writing comes from writing often and in diverse ways. Maintaining a daily journal will help to hone the students' writing skills and develop their abilities to communicate. Encourage them to reread what they have written. Try some of these ideas with your students.

- Tell the students the purpose of the journal is to give them a format for recording their thoughts and feelings about what they read, as well as to furnish them a record of their progress in writing over the school year.

- At the beginning of each daily class session, give your students a specific question to be answered at the end of the session. This will help them to focus on what is to be accomplished that day.

- Provide historical and cultural information the students need to place events into context. Emphasize the meaning of the world as Shakespeare and his contemporaries saw it, and encourage students to draw comparisons and distinctions between his world and their own.

- Use a wide variety of reading strategies, stopping occasionally to discuss events or characters as the action of the play proceeds. Frequent discussion is one way to help less able students learn from more competent ones and thus acquire greater skill in the expressive language needed for good writing.

- Define literary terms such as *plot*, *allusion*, *motivation*, and *point of view*, and record them in the journals. The students will then have a ready guide to the terms when they need them.

- Allow the use of the journals as "open books" during quizzes to encourage students to make more adequate use of them.

- If possible, keep the journals in the classroom. This will help ensure neatness, maintain availability, and alert the students that you consider journals to be an important part of their study—something to be proud of.

Cue Line

1. On the back o. ...

2. Why does Rom... ...s Juliet?

_____

_____

_____

3. Juliet asks, "Romeo, ...re he is? Explain.

_____

_____

_____

4. Why does Juliet fear that R... ...think she is "too quickly won"?

_____

_____

_____

5. What will Juliet's kinsmen do if they see her talking to Romeo?

_____

_____

6. When Friar Lawrence encounters Romeo after he has been with Juliet, he thinks the young man has been with Rosaline. Why is that?

_____

_____

_____

7. When speaking to Juliet's nurse, whom does Romeo describe in this way: "A gentleman that loves to hear himself talk"?

_____

_____

8. What does Juliet's nurse agree to help her do?

_____

_____

9. Where do Romeo and Juliet secretly agree to meet and for what purpose?

_____

_____

10. On the back of this page, describe in your own words the scene that is commonly called "the balcony scene" between Romeo and Juliet.

Handwritten note:
9:55
Bryan
I need 1 copy please. to copy room,
Mr. Ent

Observing the Oxymoron

Shakespeare loved to play with words. There has probably been no other writer of English who played with words more than he did. One result of this is that his plays are full of figurative language.

Figurative language is the intentional use or arrangement of words in ways which are different from their usual use in order to make an expression more effective. One kind of figurative language is the *simile*, in which we compare one thing to another by using the word *like* or *as*. One example of a simile is "My love is like a red, red rose," in which love is compared to a rose.

Another form of figurative language is the *metaphor*, in which we compare one thing to another by speaking of it as though it is the other. An example of a metaphor would be "My love is a red, red rose." Here we say love *is* a rose, not that it is *like it*. When Romeo says, "Juliet is the sun," he is using a metaphor.

A kind of figurative language with an unusual name is the *oxymoron*. In an oxymoron, successive words seem to contradict each other, such as the following:

- double solitaire
- strongest weakness
- make haste slowly
- pretty ugly

- grownup children
- cruel kindness
- a little big

In groups of two or three, try to find the following oxymorons in *Romeo and Juliet*. Write them in the chart below, recording the act and scene in which you found each one.

> *sweet sorrow*
>
> *loving hate*
>
> *bitter sweeting*
>
> *honorable villain*

Can you find three or more oxymorons in addition to the ones above? List them in the chart with the acts and scenes in which you found them.

Oxymoron	Act	Scene

The Art of Allusion

In the works of Shakespeare, you frequently will find characters casually referring to the names of people or creatures from the Bible or from the mythology of Greece, Rome, or the British Isles. When an author does this, we call it *allusion*; and we say the author is *alluding* to Atlas or Hercules or Jacob or whomever it is he has referred to.

The education of a gentleman, such as the one Shakespeare would have received, included a great deal of mythology. Even the common people who did not go to school would have heard many of the stories told by minstrels or balladeers. And since church attendance was mandatory in many areas of England, the people would have heard Bible stories in church as well as in morality or mystery plays and tableaus.

Storytelling has always been a favorite pastime of people who have no other entertainment, and when one of Shakespeare's characters mentions Echo or Helen of Troy or Venus, the audience would have recognized the name and related what was being said in the play to the story of that person. A modern playwright might allude to a well-known film star, a television program, or to a president of the United States in the same way.

Activities

1. In groups of two or three, research one of the following mythological persons, Bible characters, or mythological creatures to which Shakespeare alludes in *Romeo and Juliet*. Learn the story of the character or creature and write a description and explanation, briefly telling its background and story.

• Queen Mab	• Abraham	• Phoebus
• Cockatrice	• Venus	• God's Lady (the Virgin Mary)
• Dido	• Cleopatra	• Helen of Troy
• Hero	• Thisbe	• Sol
• Echo		

2. Write a skit about one of the above, dramatizing the story. Present your skit to the rest of the class and explain why you think Shakespeare may have alluded to this person or creature in the way he did.

3. In groups of two to five, research a mythological character or creature other than one of the above, and produce a mural showing an important part of its story. For this activity, you will need the following:

   • butcher paper

   • poster paints or markers

   • pencils

What's in a Name?

In Act II, Scene 2, Juliet says "What's in a name?—That which we call a rose by any other name would smell as sweet." She's in a quandary about having fallen in love with the son of her family's enemy. "Why is Romeo a Montague?" she is saying, and "Why am I a Capulet?" Names can be very important, and so they are with the names of this play's two main characters.

The play's name, *Romeo and Juliet,* is now synonymous with the idea of tragic young love, and most people in the Western world would immediately recognize their names. When the play was first performed in England, most Elizabethans also would have recognized the names, for the story of the tragic young lovers had been told many times and was familiar to them. What if the story were a new one, however? Would the title be a good one—that is, one which would draw people to the play?

When you are naming a story, book, or play, here are some guidelines to use for choosing a title which is eye-catching and effective.

1. The title must have a definite connection with the story, play, or book.

2. It must catch the interest of the reader in a compelling way.

3. It should never give away the story or reveal the solution. This will spend the reader's interest before he starts to read.

4. It must challenge the reader to want to find out what the story is about.

5. It should not be "cutesy," humorous, or alliterative (nothing like *Cool Cat Combat,* as an example).

6. It must be suitable so the reader will know right away whether the story is for a child or an adult.

When Leonard Bernstein used the plot of *Romeo and Juliet* for a musical, he changed the setting from the streets of Verona, Italy, to the streets of Spanish Harlem in New York City. In accordance with the new setting, he titled his play *West Side Story.*

Activity

Shakespeare's plays are often produced using new settings. The story may be set in Spanish Harlem in the twentieth century, as *West Side Story* is, or *Hamlet* may be set in Nazi Germany. Imagine that you are going to use the plot of *Romeo and Juliet* for a play of your own about two young lovers. Change the setting (time and place) of the story to one of your own, and then give your play a new title. Keep the basic characters—Mercutio, Tybalt, Friar Lawrence, and Nurse—but give them different names to fit into your new time and place. Use the guidelines above to help you.

New Title for *Romeo and Juliet*: _____

Setting (Time & Place):_____

Characters' Names and Descriptions: _____

_____

Love at First Sight

What would a young girl's parents think if one night she came home and announced, "Mom (and/or Dad), I've fallen in love with the boy I met at the party tonight. We want to get married tomorrow!"

They'd be horrified, right? But Romeo and Juliet decided to get married the very night they met. They couldn't tell their parents, however, because the two families were enemies; so the young lovers decided to be married secretly. Surprisingly, there were adults in their lives who helped them with the plan. Friar Lawrence and Juliet's scatterbrained nurse became co-conspirators in facilitating Romeo and Juliet's deception; and when they did this, the young people's lives were overtaken by misunderstandings. Tragedy became inevitable.

Some young people secretly dream of love at first sight. Young girls may imagine a handsome, charming young man will come suddenly into their lives, sweep them off their feet, and help them to live happily forever after. Young men may see a pretty girl and immediately be stricken by the love bug. These dreams and feelings are normal. They are the stuff of which romantic comedies and Hollywood musicals are made.

Young people in their teens, however, have many reasons to think twice before getting married so young. What do you think about this? It is wise to weigh both sides of a question before making a decision about something as important as marriage.

Activity

In the columns below, list in the plus column all the reasons you can think of in favor of getting married while still in one's teens. In the minus column, list all the reasons you can think of for not getting married while still in one's teens. After you have listed all the reasons you can think of for each column, write a paragraph stating your decision about which course of action is best, giving your reasons for believing this to be true. You may use the back of the page if you need to do so.

Plus Column	Minus Column

Quiz Time

1. On the back of this paper, list three important events in Act III.

2. Whom do Benvolio and Mercutio encounter in Scene 1?

   _____

   _____

3. When Romeo enters, what does Tybalt call him, and what is Romeo's response?

   _____

   _____

   _____

4. After Mercutio and Tybalt fight, why does Mercutio say, "tomorrow . . . you will find me a grave man"?

   _____

   _____

   _____

5. What sentence does the Prince pass on Romeo for killing Tybalt?

   _____

   _____

6. How does Juliet react to the news of Tybalt's death?

   _____

   _____

   _____

7. Who becomes the intermediary between Romeo and Juliet?

   _____

   _____

8. What "joyful tidings" does Lady Capulet bring to Juliet shortly after Romeo has left her room?

   _____

   _____

9. What choice does Capulet give his daughter?

   _____

   _____

10. Juliet says that Fortune (Fate) is fickle (changeable). On the back of this page, answer this question: Is what has happened between Mercutio, Tybalt, and Romeo something that was "written in the stars" so that nothing could have been done about it? How could this tragic situation have been prevented in some way?

Romeo and Juliet Word Search

```
Q F S H A K E S P E A R E B L L I O M L N W
W R T Y U S T R A T F O R D U P O N A V O N
E E E U I G D I O A A M O N T A G U E K B F
R E W O P H S U P Q S E N V M K I P M J N D
T L W M A N T U A W D O N C N J U L N H B Q
Y I A P L J Y U V E D A M X B H Y K B H V W
U Z S R K K B Y E R F N U R S E T J V L C E
U A D I J L A T R T G D L G A L I L E O X R
I B E N V O L I O Y H J M S D G R H V N Z T
O E G C H M T R N U J U L A V F R G C D Y T
P T F E F N A C A P U L E T C S E F X O A U
L H G S D B Q E P F R I A R L A W R E N C E
K I H A Z V W E O I J E K A X A W D Z G S I
N I J Z X C M E R C U T I O Z A Q S A F D O
```

Find the names of persons and places named by the following clues. Write the answers in the spaces to the right of the clues and outline the words as you locate them in the word search above.

- ❖ The Bard of Avon _____
- ❖ Romeo's last name _____
- ❖ Juliet's cousin _____
- ❖ Shakespeare's birthplace _____
- ❖ Star-crossed lovers _____
- ❖ Juliet's father _____
- ❖ Romeo's place of exile _____
- ❖ City of Globe Theater _____
- ❖ Talks a lot _____
- ❖ Scene of *Romeo and Juliet* _____
- ❖ He marries Romeo and Juliet _____
- ❖ Queen who sponsored Shakespeare _____
- ❖ She is with Juliet from birth. _____
- ❖ Friend of Mercutio and Romeo _____
- ❖ He sentences Romeo to exile. _____
- ❖ Astronomer sentenced for saying Earth revolves around the sun _____

Read It Trippingly on the Tongue

The words of Shakespeare are the most quoted phrases in the English language. Thousands of lines first said by him are in our everyday speech. Bartlett's *Familiar Quotations*, a book in which many people seek out oft-heard sayings, lists 88 pages in small print and double columns of quotations from Shakespeare's plays and poems! In this quotation from *Hamlet*, he even tells us through a character how to say his words:

> *Speak the speech, I pray you, as I pronounced it to you, trippingly on the tongue.*

What does that mean? In *Hamlet*, he meant not to overact, not to be what is known to us as a *ham*, a bad actor.

This passage also indicates a little of how to read his plays—clearly and precisely, without overdoing it, for that is how Shakespeare's work is to be read, if it is to be read well or to be well-read, as the case may be.

Here are some guidelines on how to read *Romeo and Juliet*.

- Before you read it, see the play if you can. There are good videos to make this easy for you. Some are listed in the bibliography of this book, but if a production is playing near you, by all means, go see it! Shakespeare wrote his plays to be performed on stage, and that's the manner in which they are best experienced. *Romeo and Juliet* is full of action as well as words.

- Read *Romeo and Juliet* aloud. Read a whole scene without looking up any of the words. You will understand more than you thought you would. If you wish, you can look the words up in the footnotes after you finish the scene.

- Don't worry about having to understand every word. Even if you don't understand every word, you will understand the play.

Activity

In groups of three to five, choose a scene and divide the parts in the scene among the members of your group. Using the guidelines above, read the scene aloud. Practice reading it aloud at least several times. Memorize it if you can. Then present your version of the scene to the class.

Which scene will you choose? One full of action, as where Mercutio or Tybalt are killed in street fights? A romantic one, such as the scene at the masquerade ball when Romeo and Juliet meet? Or a humorous one, such as when Romeo's friends encounter Nurse on the street and bedevil her?

Anne Boleyn, Mother of Queen Elizabeth I

Queen Elizabeth I, who sponsored and protected Shakespeare and his theater, was the daughter of King Henry VIII and his second wife, Anne Boleyn. The story of their short marriage is part of a long saga of a king who started his own church so he could do what he wanted to do and a queen whose life he ended when their daughter was very small.

Henry Tudor, King of England from 1509 to 1547, was well-educated and musical, often composing his own songs. Shortly before he became king, he married Catherine of Aragon, the daughter of King Ferdinand and Queen Isabella of Spain and widow of his brother Arthur. They were happy for some time, but they had only one child who lived—a daughter, Mary. It was important that a king have a son to inherit the throne. Henry's eye began to wander, and he fell in love with Anne Boleyn.

He declared his marriage had been a mistake because Catherine had been married to Henry's dead brother before he married her. The official church of England was Roman Catholic, and Henry requested the church's permission to divorce Catherine. His request was not granted soon enough to please him, so he appointed a new chief minister (Archbishop of Canterbury), Thomas Cranmer, who broke from the Roman Catholic Church and forthwith granted Henry his divorce.

Henry married Anne Boleyn, and within a year she bore him another daughter, Elizabeth, who was declared heir to the throne instead of Mary. But when Anne Boleyn did not bear Henry a son within the next three years, Henry declared that she was unfaithful, and he had her executed by beheading in 1536. Henry went on to marry four more times before he died. His only son, Edward, by his third wife, Jane Seymour, died while still a boy.

Many tales are told about Anne Boleyn, some true, some not. It is said her ghost wanders around the corridors of the Tower of London, which is where her head was removed by the executioner's axe, and some witnesses have claimed to see her carriage rolling up the drive to her childhood home, Brickling Manor. When Henry died in 1547, his only son became King Edward VI. When Edward died after a fall in 1553, the throne went to his half sister Mary, who became infamous as "Bloody Mary." When Mary was deposed, Elizabeth was crowned queen.

Activity

Research the reign of Queen Mary to learn why she became known as "Bloody Mary" and to learn about the struggles between the two daughters of Henry. Then write a biographical sketch of Queen Mary. Tell why you would, or would not, have liked to live during the times of Henry VIII, Queen Mary, and Queen Elizabeth. If you had to choose the reign of one of them in which to live, name that monarch and tell your reasons for feeling that way.

The Chorus in *Romeo and Juliet*

Two households, both alike in dignity	a
(In fair Verona, where we lay our scene),	b
From Ancient grudge break to new mutiny,	a
Where civil blood makes civil hands unclean.	b
From forth the fatal loins of these two foes	c
A pair of star-crossed lovers take their life;	d
Whose misadventured piteous overthrows	c
Doth with their death bury their parents' strife.	d
The fearful passage of their death-marked love	e
And the continuance of their parents' rage,	f
Which, but their children's end, naught could remove,	e
Is now the two hours' traffic of our stage;	f
The which, if you with patient ears attend,	g
What here shall miss, our toil shall strive to mend.	g

Usually a writer bends over backward to avoid letting the reader know the outcome of the story ahead of time. It is said that if a writer releases too much of the plot of a story too soon, the reader will not care to read any further. Yet here is one of the greatest of all English writers telling us at the beginning of a play that our two young lovers will die because of their parents' anger and wish for revenge. He is giving us a warning of what can happen to innocent people caught in the web of someone else's hate.

The use of a chorus to comment on the action of a play was a familiar literary device in ancient drama. The old Greek plays of Sophocles, for example, usually had a chorus commenting throughout the play about what was happening and making judgments of whether the characters could have done other than what they did in the play. The Ancient Greeks believed that all events were planned by the gods and that man, no matter how noble, could not change the course of fate. The Greek chorus continually pointed out the proofs of this during a play.

Activity

Acts I and II begin with a chorus reciting in the form of a sonnet what is happening and what is going to happen. Act III, however, does not begin with a chorus, nor do Acts IV and V. After reading Act III, write a chorus to be recited at the beginning of the act. If you enjoy writing poetry and would like to try writing your chorus in the form of a sonnet, by all means do so. The rhyme scheme for a sonnet may be found to the right of the box above. If you are more comfortable writing prose, write your chorus in prose.

Quiz Time

1. On the back of this paper, list three important events from Act IV.

2. What does County Paris plan to do on Thursday?

   _____

   _____

3. From whom does Juliet ask help?

   _____

   _____

4. What does Friar Lawrence plan to do to prevent County Paris from accomplishing his goal?

   _____

   _____

   _____

5. How will Juliet spend Wednesday night if all goes as planned?

   _____

   _____

   _____

6. Where is Romeo during all of the above?

   _____

   _____

7. What does Juliet tell her father when she returns home on Tuesday?

   _____

   _____

   _____

8. List two reasons Juliet does not want to follow her father's wishes.

   _____

   _____

   _____

9. When Nurse goes to Juliet's chamber to wake her in the morning, what does she find?

   _____

   _____

10. Juliet's nurse and Friar Lawrence go out of their way trying to help Romeo and Juliet, but they make some terrible mistakes. On the back of this page, discuss the mistakes they made. Do you think they could, or should, have done differently?

Experiments with Air

Aristotle taught that everything in the world was made up of four elements—fire, earth, water, and air—and that differences in things existed because these elements were present in differing amounts in different things. Because Aristotle had said so, Shakespeare and his contemporaries also believed this.

Air is all around you. It is in your bedroom at home, in your classroom at school, and outside. We take it for granted. You can't see it or touch it. Therefore it does not weigh anything, and it does not take up space. Right? Wrong!

Conduct these experiments to prove that air has weight and takes up space.

Weighing Air

Materials Needed:

- a stick
- a pencil with straight sides
- string
- two identical balloons
- transparent tape
- two cans

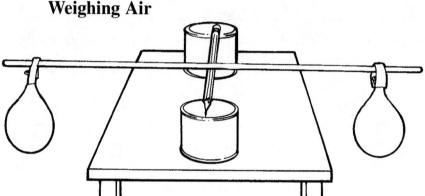

Directions:

1. Mark the exact middle of your stick.

2. Rest the pencil between cans and balance the middle of the stick across the pencil so it is level.

3. Check the weight of the balloons by taping each to one end of the stick. If the stick remains level, they weigh the same.

4. Unstick one balloon and blow it up.

5. Restick the balloon to the end of the stick. Does the stick now remain level?

Explanation: *When you stuck a filled balloon on the end of the stick, that end went down because it weighs more than the empty balloon. When you blow air into the balloon, it fills, showing that air takes up space.*

Heating and Cooling Air

Materials Needed:

- a plastic bottle
- a balloon
- a deep bowl
- hot water
- ice

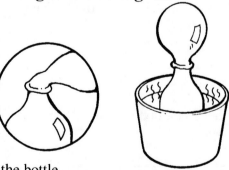

Directions:

1. Fit the balloon over the mouth of the bottle.

2. Stand the bottle in a bowl and fill the bowl with hot water. What happens?

3. Pour out the hot water and fill the bowl with ice. What happens now?

Explanation: *When hot water warms the air in the bottle, it expands to fill space in the balloon. When ice cools the air in the bottle, it contracts and takes up less space as the balloon deflates.*

Shakespearean Superstitions

The people of Shakespeare's time were very superstitious. Superstitions usually have their beginnings with people who are uneducated and ignorant. They do not know or understand many things that happen, so they attribute magical qualities to puzzling occurrences as a way of explaining them. Some of the superstitions the Elizabethans believed include the following:

- If the bay trees (laurels) wither, you'll know the king has died.
- If two friends are walking together and a child or animal walks between them, they will stop being friends.
- If you wish, you can tell what kind of person someone is by knowing on which day of the week that person was born, according to the following:

> *Monday's child is fair in face.*
> *Tuesday's child is full of grace.*
> *Wednesday's child is full of woe.*
> *Thursday's child has far to go.*
> *Friday's child is loving and giving.*
> *Saturday's child works hard for a living.*
> *A child born on Christmas day is fair and wise and good.*
> (What about Sunday's child? Nothing was said!)

- If the family has mutton (sheep) for dinner and finds a spot on the blade bone after the meat has been picked from it, there will be a funeral in the family.
- If you wish to find a person who has drowned, throw a loaf of bread into the water near where he drowned, and it will go directly over the body.
- If you do not throw bones into the fire, you will not get a toothache.
- If you give milk to a strange woman, she might be a witch who will use that milk to bewitch your cow.
- If you give holy bread and holy water to your horse, no one will steal it.
- If the sun shines on the day of a wedding, the bride will always be happy.

Activity

In groups of three or four, ask family members, teachers, and friends any superstitions they know about any of the following:

- black cats
- salt
- fire
- sun
- devil
- birthdays
- ladders
- babies
- moon
- spiders
- knots
- mirrors
- dropping or spilling something
- stars
- days of the week or month
- falling

Then come together and list the ones you collected. Decide which ones are the strangest, discuss them, and write any explanations you can think of for them. Share your ideas with the class.

Alchemy

During Shakespeare's time there was no science as we know it today. So-called scientists then practiced what they called *alchemy*, and they were concerned with trying to turn common metals into gold by a process called *transmutation*. They thought that if they could do this, they would discover a single cure for all diseases and be able to prolong life indefinitely.

Alchemy began in ancient China and Egypt and grew into a sort of mystical belief which was surrounded by superstitions. Aristotle had taught that everything was composed of four elements—fire, air, water, and earth, and if one could find the secret key to their composition, it would be possible to change copper or lead or any other metal into gold. Alchemists spent their entire lives trying to discover this key.

It was not until the nineteenth century that chemistry progressed to the point of defining an element as a substance that could not be broken down into simpler ones. The known number of such substances began to increase rapidly as scientists discovered one element after another. They soon noticed that the elements each had certain properties and that they could be grouped together into families which shared these characteristics. This led to what is called *periodic law*.

In 1870 the first periodic table of the elements was published. On this table, the elements are arranged according to their atomic weights. The table has been added to and rearranged as scientists have learned more about the earth and all its elements. The table helped scientists discover nuclear energy, and it gives them a tool to help predict what will happen in a given experiment.

The discovery of many elements and their classification has not helped scientists to end death, but it has enabled them to prolong the average life expectancy and to eliminate many diseases which once killed people while they were still young. And, surprisingly, it is now possible to transmute common metals into gold. However, the process is very expensive and not worth the cost.

Activity

Aristotle thought air was an element of and by itself, but it is not. Air is about 78% nitrogen and 21% oxygen. Fire, which is not an element, requires oxygen to burn. You can learn the importance of oxygen to fire with the following experiment. Do this with an adult present to supervise.

Set three identical candles in saucers with modeling clay and place them in a safe place, such as on a firm table or on a counter. Light the candles and place a large jar over one, a small jar over one, and leave one in the open. Which candle goes out first, which second, and which continues to burn? What conclusion can you draw from this? Write your responses below or on the back of this page.

Write a Diary

These past few days have been very intense for Romeo and Juliet. They have met, fallen in love, and married. Romeo has seen the murder of his friend Mercutio, and Romeo himself has killed Tybalt. Can you imagine how each of them feels, all the emotions which are running through them? Remember, they are only 14 and 15, and although they were considered more adult then than they would be now (partly because people did not live so long then), still they are very young and must be very scared.

Imagine that you are either Romeo or Juliet, and you need to deal with all the strong feelings you have at this moment. Write a diary entry for each of the past three days. Describe all that has happened to you and how you feel about it. And describe the way you feel about this wonderful person who has come into your life and the complications that have come into your life as well. What will you say?

Dear Diary,

Quiz Time

1. On the back of this paper, list three important events from Act V.

2. Where is Romeo at the beginning of Act V?

   _____

   _____

3. How does Romeo feel? What does he believe is going to happen?

   _____

   _____

   _____

4. What news does Balthasar bring to Romeo?

   _____

   _____

5. Why has Friar Lawrence given a letter to Friar John to deliver to Romeo?

   _____

   _____

6. Where does Romeo confront Paris, and what happens?

   _____

   _____

7. Why does Romeo take poison?

   _____

   _____

8. When Juliet sees Romeo's body lying next to her, what does she do?

   _____

   _____

9. How does Friar Lawrence explain the tragic event to the Prince?

   _____

   _____

   _____

10. Choose one of these statements, and on the back of this page write your responses to it.

    • *Juliet was owned by her parents, and she had to die to be free of their wishes.*

    • *Juliet was owned by herself, and she died because she chose to do so.*

Make a Sundial

Clocks as we know them were not invented until near the time of Shakespeare's birth, but people have had many different ways of judging the passage of time. They could tell the approximate time of day by the position of the sun in the sky. The Chinese had a water clock which indicated time by the flowing of water or with a moving float. In 1580 Galileo, the same man who was sentenced to life in prison for saying the Earth moved around the sun, suggested that the regular movement of a pendulum could control the hands of a clock, but it was another 70 years before such a clock was invented. Now we have watches and clocks controlled by tiny microprocessors which run seemingly forever without having to be wound or reset.

The Europeans of Shakespeare's time used sundials to tell the time. You can make a sundial on your own. Of course, you will only be able to use it on sunny days and never at night.

Materials Needed:

- a piece of stiff cardboard

- a protractor

- a 12" (30 cm) square piece of wood or heavy pasteboard

Directions:

1. Using the protractor to measure the angle, cut a right-angle triangular piece (6 inches x 4 inches, or 15 cm x 10 cm) from the stiff cardboard. This part is called the *gnomon*.

2. Tape the gnomon upright on the wooden block, with the long side as the base.

3. Place the sundial on a flat surface outdoors with the triangle's highest point facing directly north. Early in the day, every hour on the hour draw a line where the shadow of the gnomon falls. Write down the hour at each line. Now you can tell by looking at the sundial when it is time to go to lunch or to go home.

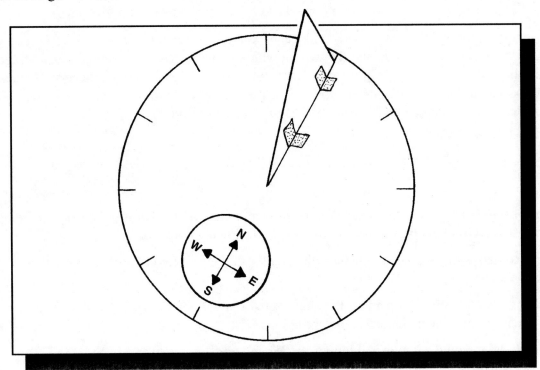

The Differences Between Comedy and Tragedy

Most plays are either comedies or tragedies, although Shakespeare also wrote histories. The dictionary defines *comedy* as a play or movie "of light and humorous character with a happy ending." It defines *tragedy* as "a play dealing with a serious or somber theme—that of a great person destined through a flaw of character or conflict with some overpowering force to suffer downfall or destruction." *Romeo and Juliet*, as it is written, is a tragedy.

Aristotle, the same man who said the sun, planets, and stars revolve around the Earth, said that we see persons as funny when we think we are better than they are, because we can laugh at them without feeling sorry for them. He also said that tragedy is about noble characters for whom we feel pity.

Some modern writers have said that the only differences between comedy and tragedy are that a comedy ends happily, while a tragedy ends unhappily.

There are many reasons that *Romeo and Juliet*, except for its unhappy (tragic) ending, could be played as a comedy. Some of the situations are silly—even ridiculous—such as the encounter between Juliet's nurse and Romeo, Benvolio, and Mercutio. The characters all misinterpret or misunderstand what is happening, much as the characters in a slapstick comedy do. And Romeo himself is in many ways funny. His falling in love at first sight with Juliet when he supposedly was already madly in love with Rosaline provides a perfect scenario for a comedy. We might even call him girl-crazy.

There is a very thin line between comedy and tragedy, and the director of *Romeo and Juliet* must carefully direct what the actors do and the way in which they speak so the ending is truly tragic. If Romeo is allowed to be too funny in the early acts, when the play ends the audience will not see the deaths of the young lovers as tragic because they will not have learned in the course of the play to empathize with them. People do not usually feel pity for a buffoon.

Activity

In groups of three or four, rewrite the ending of *Romeo and Juliet* so that it becomes a comedy rather than a tragedy. Before you begin, ask yourselves the following questions:

1. Will Romeo and Juliet need to behave differently in the first two acts of the play than they would in a tragedy?

2. Will you need to eliminate any of the characters or situations to make the play funny, or can you do it with all the same characters and situations?

3. Exactly how would a happy and humorous *Romeo and Juliet* end?

The Struggle for Truth

We all know that Earth and the other planets rotate around the sun, don't we? When we all know a thing to be factually true, we often assume that everyone else also knows what we know and that they always have known it. But in Shakespeare's time, the people of Europe did not know much of what we know. For one thing, they thought the sun went around the earth and that the stars and the planets did also.

For over a thousand years the Western World believed in a theory about the earth, moon, sun, and stars, called *Ptolemaic astronomy*. It was named after Ptolemy, a Greek astronomer who lived in the first century A.D. Ptolemy postulated a mathematical system of the motions of sun, moon, and planets on the framework first supplied by a Greek philosopher named Aristotle. This framework said that the earth was the center of the universe and that the sun and the stars revolved around it. No one challenged this idea because the church said that it fit with what was in the Bible.

In 1543, however, a Polish astronomer named Copernicus published a manuscript that said an earth which rotated with the other planets around a central sun could explain what was known about the movements of the heavens better than a sun which rotated around the earth. This *heliocentric* (sun-centered) theory of Copernicus' was not widely known by the Elizabethans, however, and they continued in their beliefs.

While Shakespeare was writing his plays, unknown to him an Italian astronomer named Galileo was building a new telescope and watching the heavens through it. In 1610, the year Shakespeare retired to Stratford-upon-Avon, Galileo decided that Copernicus had been right. The earth did revolve around the sun! In 1615 he wrote a letter saying scientists should be granted the right to freely seek the truth, but in 1616 the church ordered him to stop telling his lies that the earth revolved around the sun. Nevertheless, he continued to say it, and in 1633 he was sentenced to life imprisonment for "vehement suspicion of heresy."

In the meantime, many people of Shakespeare's time based much of what they believed about each other, what happened to them, and their physical ailments on the movements of the sun and stars around the earth. Shakespeare wrote the following in *King Lear*:

> *"It is the stars,*
> *The stars above us, govern our conditions."*

This belief is echoed throughout the plays of Shakespeare. It would be a mistake, of course, to assume that Shakespeare himself believed everything he has his characters say. A very famous line in *Julius Caesar*, for example, has Cassius saying,

> *"The fault, dear Brutus, is not in our stars,*
> *but in ourselves, that we are underlings."*

To many Elizabethans, astrology was not just fun. It was the science which governed the universe.

Activity

Complete the activity on page 36, Shakespeare in the Solar System.

The Struggle for Truth *(cont.)*

Shakespeare in the Solar System

Assume that Mercutio (who is *really* an alien from the planet Mercury) is not really killed in the duel with Tybalt. He uses his regenerative powers to return to life to help Romeo and Juliet escape from Verona to a better place—another planet, in fact. He offers to transport the amazed couple to his planet or any other in the solar system if they choose. Because of differences in planet sizes and orbits, Mercutio explains, certain changes in figuring a person's age and weight will take place. Mercutio supplies them with the data they will need to compute those changes. Follow his directions based on the data and do the calculations for some surprising results.

	Mercury	Venus	Earth	Mars	Jupiter	Saturn	Uranus	Neptune	Pluto
Length of Year (trip around the sun)	88 days	224.7 days	365.3 days	687 days	11.86 years	29.46 years	84 years	165 years	248 years
Gravity at Surface	.38 g	.91 g	1.00 g	.38 g	2.53 g	1.07 g	.91 g	1.16 g	.05 g
Juliet's Age			14						
Juliet's Weight			110						
Romeo's Age			15						
Romeo's Weight			135						

Use the formula below to calculate the lovers' ages on each planet.

$$\underset{\text{age in years}}{\underline{\hspace{3cm}}} \times 365 = \underset{\text{age in days}}{\underline{\hspace{3cm}}} \div \underset{\text{planet's year in days}}{\underline{\hspace{3cm}}} = \underset{\text{age on this planet}}{\underline{\hspace{3cm}}}$$

Use the formula below to calculate the lovers' weight on each planet.

$$\underset{\text{weight on Earth}}{\underline{\hspace{3cm}}} \times \underset{\text{gravity at surface on this planet}}{\underline{\hspace{3cm}}} = \underset{\text{weight on this planet}}{\underline{\hspace{3cm}}}$$

Challenge: Using the data above, compute your own age and weight on each of the planets in our solar system.

To the Teacher:

Fold this answer key under or cover it before reproducing the above activity.

	Mercury	Venus	Earth	Mars	Jupiter	Saturn	Uranus	Neptune	Pluto
Length of Year (trip around the sun)	88 days	224.7 days	365.3 days	687 days	11.86 years	29.46 years	84 years	165 years	248 years
Gravity at Surface	.38 g	.91 g	1.00g	.38 g	2.53 g	1.07 g	.91 g	1.16 g	.05 g
Juliet's Age	58	22.7	14	7.4	1.18	.47	.16	.08	.05
Juliet's Weight	41.8	100	110	42	278	118	100	128	5.5
Romeo's Age	62.7	24	15	8	1.26	.50	.17	.09	.06
Romeo's Weight	51	123	135	51.3	342	144	123	157	6.7

Writing Couplets

Writing poetry was an important part of being an educated person in Elizabethan England. In fact, when Shakespeare first began writing plays, he was both a poet and a playwright, for almost all plays were written in rhythmic (but not necessarily rhymed) verse in those days. *Romeo and Juliet* was one of his earliest plays, and it is full of poetry. As soon as Romeo falls in love with Juliet, everything he says to her or about her is in verse. He gave a whole new voice to the idea of romantic love.

There were two main forms of poetry which were popular. One form enjoyed by everyone, even those who were not educated, was the *ballad*. A ballad told a story in verses (or stanzas) of four lines each. Today's songwriters sometimes write songs in the form of ballads. Many country and western lyrics are in ballad form. One kind of ballad popular in Elizabethan England was the news ballad, sort of a musical gossip tabloid with which a balladeer or minstrel would go from town to town singing or telling a sensational story which had happened in another town.

The form of poetry most prized by an educated person, however, was the *sonnet*. A sonnet was a very stylized poem of 14 lines with a standard rhyme scheme that varied little (see page 26). Sometimes sonnets were strung together to form a narrative. The last two lines of a sonnet rhyme with each other and are, therefore, called a *couplet*. Here are two couplets from Shakespeare sonnets. The first one is from the chorus in Act II of *Romeo and Juliet*.

> *But passion lends them power, time means, to meet,*
> *Temp'ring extremities with extreme sweet.*

> *For we, which now behold these present days,*
> *Have eyes to wonder, but lack tongues to praise.*

Activity

One at a time, read each of the 24 scenes of *Romeo and Juliet* and select four that you understand or like the best. Then, for each scene write an original couplet which expresses what happens. Try to catch the feeling of the scene and see how many different ways you can find to make your couplet rhyme. Place your completed couplets below.

My Couplets

Act_____ Scene_____	_____
Act_____ Scene_____	_____
Act_____ Scene_____	_____
Act_____ Scene_____	_____

Any Questions?

When you finished reading *Romeo and Juliet*, did you have any questions? Write some of your questions on the back of this page.

Work in groups or by yourself to prepare possible answers for some or all of the questions you have asked above and those written below. When you have finished your responses, share your ideas with the class.

The Relationship

❖ Was Romeo girl-crazy before he met Juliet?

❖ Why did he fall out of love so quickly with Rosaline just to fall in love with Juliet?

❖ Was Romeo really just a silly boy who couldn't make up his mind, or did he change because of Juliet?

❖ Why did Romeo begin to speak in poetry when he met Juliet? Had Juliet ever met any other boys besides her relatives before she met Romeo?

❖ If Juliet hadn't met and fallen in love with Romeo, would she have fallen in love with Paris instead?

❖ Are arranged marriages (such as Capulet wanted to make for his daughter) good in the long run since they are thought out rationally to benefit the whole family, or are marriages for love better? Explain.

The Feud

❖ How did the blood feud between the Montagues and the Capulets get started?

❖ If Mercutio had turned his back on Tybalt and walked away when Tybalt was trying to provoke a fight, would Tybalt have given up the fight?

❖ Was there any way that Tybalt and Mercutio would have refused to fight each other when Romeo tried to get them to stop?

❖ If Romeo had followed his own advice and not fought Tybalt after Mercutio's killing, what would the Montagues have done to him? to Tybalt?

❖ Was the deadly fight between Romeo and Tybalt inevitable?

Nurse and Friar Lawrence

❖ Should Nurse and Friar Lawrence have agreed to help Romeo and Juliet get married?

❖ Why would Nurse keep such a secret from the family she had worked for all those years?

❖ Why should a priest have married two young people who had known each other only one day?

❖ How could Romeo and Juliet have found happiness in marriage without all the secrecy?

❖ If you had been Nurse, what would you have advised Juliet to do about Romeo?

❖ If you had been Friar Lawrence, what would you have advised Romeo to do about Romeo?

Dreams

❖ What does Mercutio mean by saying that dreams are the children of an idle brain? Do you agree with him? Why or why not?

Book Report Ideas

Good pieces of literature may be reported on in many ways. After reading *Romeo and Juliet*, use one of the following suggestions for your report or choose another of your own which you would prefer.

- Choose a passage from the play which you really like or choose a soliloquy from another of Shakespeare's plays. Memorize the passage and learn as much as you can about where the passage falls in the play and what its importance is to the play. Then recite it for the class.

- Choose a scene from the play and with one or more of your classmates learn it and present a dramatization of it for the class.

- Make a model of the Globe Theater where Shakespeare's plays were first produced. Research its history and present an oral presentation to the class about it.

- Construct a diorama of a scene you especially like in the play. Include scenery and characters in your scene. Research Elizabethan clothing to ensure that your characters are dressed in line with the times in which the play takes place.

- Compile an Elizabethan poetry book. Choose poems of the era which you particularly enjoy and put them into a book which you illustrate. You might include some of Shakespeare's sonnets, but you also might include poems of other Elizabethan poets.

- Make a poster to invite people to a class showing of *Romeo and Juliet.* Include in your poster a favorite scene from the play and tell something exciting or enjoyable about it which you think would gain the interest of others.

- Rewrite a scene from the play in modern English and with an appropriate number of your classmates present your dramatization of the scene.

- Become a tour guide to Stratford-upon-Avon. Learn as much as you can about the town in which Shakespeare was born and give your classmates a "tour" of the town, telling your audience some of the town's history as you go along.

- Research an aspect of the history of English drama. For example, many of your classmates might be surprised to learn that there were no actresses in Shakespeare's time, only actors. Boys and young men played the parts of girls and women. Someone at the time said that no woman could play the part of a girl as well as a certain boy actor. What do you think of that?

- Write an alternative play. Ask yourself, "What if something in the play had been different?" How would it have been? Rewrite the play with this difference, showing the way that difference causes another outcome.

Research Ideas

Describe three things in *Romeo and Juliet* that you would like to learn more about.

1. _____

2. _____

3. _____

Romeo and Juliet may be the first Shakespeare play you have read. Shakespeare was a very productive writer, and his plays are full of allusions to history, mythology, and the Bible which may be strange to you. Researching some of the people, places, and stories which he and his audiences of 400 years ago instantly recognized can help you more thoroughly understand this play and give you a better appreciation of Shakespeare's incredible craftsmanship as a writer.

In small groups or on your own, research one or more of the topics listed below. Then share what you have discovered with the class.

- Queen Elizabeth I
- King Henry VIII
- Geoffrey Chaucer
- London Bridge
- The Puritans
- William Caxton and the printing press
- English explorers in the New World
- Greek mythology
- The church in fifteenth century England
- The London Bear Garden
- English castles
- London hospitals
- The spice trade
- English royalty and nobility
- Robert, Earl of Essex
- Anne Boleyn
- Shakespeare sonnets
- Stratford-upon-Avon
- The Tower of London
- The Protestant Reformation
- "Bloody Mary" Tudor
- Roman mythology
- Elizabethan education
- Great Elizabethan houses
- Timber-framed houses
- The hue and cry
- The Spanish Armada
- Elizabethan child-raising practices
- Shakespeare histories

- Elizabethan London
- Lady Jane Grey
- Epic poetry
- Bubonic plague
- Women in the theater
- Thomas à Becket
- History of drama
- History of the English language
- Elizabethan clothing
- The great ships
- English navy during Elizabethan times
- Sir Francis Drake
- Morality and mystery plays
- Shakespeare tragedies
- Mary, Queen of Scots
- English pirates
- Ballads
- The Globe Theater
- Witch-hunting
- Sir Walter Raleigh
- Sir Francis Bacon
- The Middle Ages
- Elizabethan medicine
- Elizabethan crime and punishment
- Eton College
- Care of the poor
- Canterbury Cathedral
- Elizabethan music and dance

Fish and Chips and Shakespeare

At the end of an extensive unit such as this one on *Romeo and Juliet,* it is good to culminate with a celebration which includes parents and other classes as well as the class doing the study. It can be a time to share with others what has been learned and a time to share food and good spirits. A banquet or masquerade is one way to celebrate a Shakespeare unit, but such a celebration involves a great deal of work on the part of many people. An easier festivity to put together is one with fish and chips.

Fish and chips are the traditional "fast food" of England, natural eatables for an island country. No one knows when the custom of eating crispy fried fish together with shoestring potatoes began, but the English have enjoyed it for many generations. What Americans call French fries, the English call *chips.* (American potato chips are called *crisps* by the English.) The English like their fish and chips liberally sprinkled with malt vinegar, and when purchased at a streetside stand, they come wrapped in paper. Australian fish and chips are similar to those consumed by their English predecessors.

All you need for a fish and chips feast are frozen fried fish filets and French fries from the supermarket, some cole slaw, condiments, and an oven or microwave. A nice finishing touch might be added by providing the English dessert called trifle (a rich sponge cake served with whipped cream, custard, or fruit). Display the projects you have produced while studying *Romeo and Juliet,* perform part or all of the play for your audience, and you're in business. Here are some suggestions for activities to make your festival a roaring success.

Menu

fried fish filets   French fried potatoes   cole slaw

assorted condiments: malt vinegar, lemon slices,

catsup (called tomato sauce in England)

assorted cold drinks

trifle

Prepare frozen fish filets and potatoes according to directions on the packages. Purchase cole slaw from a deli and ask for volunteer students to prepare the simple dessert from the following recipe.

Trifle

Ingredients:
- sponge cake or pound cake cut in 1" (2.5 cm) cubes
- two bananas, sliced
- strawberries cut in half or cherries (pitted)
- vanilla pudding from a mix
- cubed fruit gelatin if desired
- whipped cream or non-dairy topping
- chopped nuts for topping if desired

Directions:

Layer the first five (four, if gelatin is not used) ingredients one half at a time in a large glass bowl. Refrigerate for one hour. Serve in individual dishes. It's simply delicious!

Activities and Displays

Activities

- ❖ Production of *Romeo and Juliet*
- ❖ Oral presentations about tragedy and comedy
- ❖ Readers' theater of Shakespearean plays and Elizabethan poetry
- ❖ Presentations of soliloquies
- ❖ Dramatizations of rewritten Shakespeare
- ❖ Dramatizations of *Romeo and Juliet* turned into comedy
- ❖ Student impersonation of Shakespeare talking about one of his plays
- ❖ Production of student-written one-act plays
- ❖ Showing one or more films of Shakespeare plays
- ❖ Oral presentation of oxymorons
- ❖ Skits dramatizing stories of mythology
- ❖ Oral discussions of pluses and minuses of love at first sight
- ❖ Oral presentations of scenes from the play
- ❖ Demonstrations of experiments with air
- ❖ Oral readings of couplets
- ❖ Oral "tour" of Stratford-upon-Avon
- ❖ Eating fish and chips
- ❖ Inviting drama students or staff from local college to present scenes from Shakespeare plays

Displays

- ❖ Illustrated dictionaries
- ❖ Glossaries of words used in drama
- ❖ Descriptions and pictures of Elizabethan clothing
- ❖ Elizabethan poetry books
- ❖ Elizabethan costumes
- ❖ Posters advertising *Romeo and Juliet*
- ❖ Research projects
- ❖ Posters illustrating Shakespeare's world
- ❖ Venn diagrams of Shakespeare's world and ours
- ❖ Response journals
- ❖ Chart of chronology of Shakespeare's plays
- ❖ Pictures of animals from vocabulary words
- ❖ Time machine descriptions
- ❖ Murals of mythological creatures and characters
- ❖ New settings and titles of *Romeo and Juliet*
- ❖ Biographical sketches of Bloody Mary
- ❖ Explanations of old superstitions
- ❖ Diaries of Romeo and Juliet
- ❖ Sundials
- ❖ Solar system displays
- ❖ Couplets

Unit Test One: Objective Test and Essay

Matching: Match the descriptions of characters with their names.

1. Friar John	_____	a.	Killed by Romeo
2. Nurse	_____	b.	Neglected to carry a message
3. Friar Lawrence	_____	c.	Juliet inspired his poetic nature
4. Prince	_____	d.	Talked a lot about nothing
5. Juliet	_____	e.	Carried the bad news to Mantua
6. Capulet	_____	f.	Intended to choose Juliet's husband for her
7. Balthasar	_____	g.	Ruled Verona
8. Romeo	_____	h.	Wished her lover had a different name
9. Benvolio	_____	i.	Supplied a potion to Juliet
10. Mercutio	_____	j.	Has raised Juliet since she was born
11. Tybalt	_____	k.	Died outside a grave
12. Paris	_____	l.	Friend of Romeo

True or False: Answer true or false in the blanks below.

1. _____ Friar Lawrence and Nurse did all the right things to help Romeo and Juliet.

2. _____ The Capulets were understanding of Juliet's wishes.

3. _____ Tybalt determined to kill Romeo.

4. _____ The Prince was the only voice of reason in *Romeo and Juliet.*

5. _____ *Romeo and Juliet* dramatizes what can happen when hate and vengeance take hold.

Short Answer: Write a brief response to each question in the space provided.

1. Who loves Juliet like her own child? _____

2. List three reasons Romeo and Juliet's love was doomed. _____

_____

_____

3. How does Friar Lawrence deceive the Capulets? _____

4. Where does *Romeo and Juliet* take place? _____

5. Why does Juliet stab herself? _____

Essay: Do you agree that Romeo and Juliet were victims of their parents and their time? Answer this question and explain why you do, or do not, agree. Give specific examples to illustrate your view.

Unit Test 2: Response

Explain the meanings of these quotations from *Romeo and Juliet*. (Be sure to tell who is speaking, who is being spoken to, and what the situation and circumstances are.)

Act I

1. *"A pair of star-crossed lovers take their life;"*
2. *"But woo her, gentle Paris, get her heart;*
   My will to her consent is but a part."
3. *"Oh, she doth teach the torches to burn bright!"*
4. *"My only love sprung from my only hate."*

Act II

1. *"But soft, what light through yonder window breaks?"*
2. *"O Romeo, Romeo, wherefore art thou Romeo?"*
3. *"Good night, good night. Parting is such sweet sorrow."*
4. *"Then hie you hence to Friar Lawrence' cell."*

Act III

1. *"Thou art a villain."*
2. *"Immediately we do exile him hence."*
3. *"Take him and cut him out in little stars,*
   And he will make the face of heaven so fine
   That all the world will be in love with night."
4. *"I'll go to Friar to know his remedy."*

Act IV

1. *"On Thursday, sir? The time is very short."*
2. *"And if thou darest, I'll give thee remedy."*
3. *"Here's drink. I drink to thee."*
4. *"Come, is the bride ready to go to church?"*

Act V

1. *"Hast thou no letters to me from the Friar?"*
2. *"I could not send it (here it is again)."*
3. *"Sweet flower, with flowers thy bridal bed I strew."*
4. *"What's here? A cup closed in my true love's hand?"*

Unit Test 3: Conversations

In size-appropriate groups, write and perform the conversation that might have occurred in one of the following situations. If you wish, you may use your own conversation idea for characters from *Romeo and Juliet*.

❖ Rosaline tells Romeo why she does not respond to his love.

❖ The Prince sits down with Mercutio and Tybalt before they have their fight and tells them why they must try to settle their differences.

❖ Nurse confesses to Lady Capulet that Juliet is in love with Romeo and that they want to get married.

❖ Lady Capulet has a quiet talk with her husband in which she takes the side of Romeo and their daughter, trying to convince him to let them marry.

❖ Friar Lawrence tells the young lovers why he cannot marry them and discusses with them the possibility of their throwing themselves on their parents' mercy.

❖ Nurse has a talk with Juliet, telling her she cannot sneak around with her and take her part against her parents.

❖ Nurse and Friar Lawrence discuss ways in which they can convince Romeo and Juliet that it is unwise to go against their parents' wishes regarding marriage.

❖ The Prince meets with both fathers to consider ending the family feud before something dreadful happens.

❖ Juliet admits to Paris that she is married to Romeo and cannot consider marrying him.

❖ Romeo goes to Capulet and asks for Juliet's hand in marriage.

❖ Lady Capulet and Lady Montague meet alone to discuss ways in which they might persuade their husbands to make peace with each other.

❖ The Prince and both sets of parents sit down for a long conversation after the deaths of Romeo and Juliet to consider other ways they could have managed their disagreements.

❖ Nurse and Friar Lawrence discuss how else they might have handled the situation of Romeo and Juliet's being in love.

❖ Benvolio, the Prince, Nurse, and Friar Lawrence each speak at the funeral of Romeo and Juliet and then discuss their eulogies later.

Chronology of Shakespeare's Plays

Titus Andronicus, 1588–1594

The Comedy of Errors, 1588–1594

Henry VI, Part 1, 1590–1591

Henry VI, Part 2, 1590–1591

Henry VI, Part 3, 1590–1591

The Taming of the Shrew, 1590

Two Gentlemen of Verona, 1590–1595

King John, 1591

Richard III, 1592

Love's Labour's Lost, 1593

Romeo and Juliet, 1593–1596

A Midsummer Night's Dream, 1595–1596

The Merchant of Venice, 1596–1598

Richard II, 1595–1596

Henry IV, Part 1, 1596–1597

Henry IV, Part 2, 1597–1598

The Merry Wives of Windsor, 1597

Much Ado About Nothing, 1598

Henry V, 1599

Julius Caesar, 1599

As You Like It, 1600

Twelfth Night, 1599–1601

Hamlet, 1600

Troilus and Cressida, 1602

All's Well That Ends Well, 1602–1604

Measure for Measure, 1603–1604

Othello, 1604

King Lear, 1606

Macbeth, 1606

Timon of Athens, 1606

Anthony and Cleopatra, 1608

Pericles, Prince of Tyre, 1607–1608

(possibly written with a collaborator)

Coriolanus, 1609

Cymbeline, 1609–1610

The Winter's Tale, 1610–1611

The Tempest, 1611

The Two Noble Kinsmen, 1613

(with John Fletcher)

Henry VIII, 1613

(with John Fletcher)

Bibliography of Related Materials

Resources

Ayto, John. *Dictionary of Word Origins*. Arcade Publishing, Little Brown and Company, 1990.

Bartlett, John. *Familiar Quotations*. Little, Brown and Company, 1955.

Birch, Beverly. *Shakespeare's Stories*. (series) Peter Bedrick Books, 1991.

Burdett, Lois. *A Child's Portrait of Shakespeare*. Black Moss Press, 1995.

Chute, Marchette. *An Introduction to Shakespeare*. Scholastic Inc., E.P. Dutton and Company, 1979.

Davidson, Diane, editor. *Romeo and Juliet for Young People*. (Series Volume 2) Swan Books, 1986.

—-*Shakespeare on Stage*. (Series Volume 3). Swan Books, 1983.

Epstein, Norrie. *The Friendly Shakespeare*. Viking Penguin, 1993.

Foster, C. *Shakespeare for Children—Romeo and Juliet*. Distributors Group, 1989.

Frye, Roland Mushat. *Shakespeare's Life and Times*. Princeton University Press, New Jersey, 1967.

Garfield, L. *Shakespeare Stories*, (2 volumes). Houghton-Mifflin, 1991.

Gibson, Rex, editor. *Romeo and Juliet* (Cambridge School Shakespeare Series). Cambridge University Press, 1992.

Harrison, G.B., editor. *Shakespeare—The Complete Works*. Harcourt, Brace & World, 1968.

Holland, Clive. *Things Seen in Shakespeare's Country*. Seely, Service & Company Limited, no date.

Horizon Magazine. *Shakespeare's England*. Harper & Row, 1964.

Lamb, Charles and Mary. *Tales from Shakespeare*. Weathervane Books, 1975.

Price, George R. *Reading Shakespeare's Plays*. Barrons Educational Series, Woodbury, 1962.

Robbins, Mari Lu. *Shakespeare, Interdisciplinary Unit*. Teacher Created Resources, 1995.

Ross, S. *Shakespeare and Macbeth*. Penguin, 1994.

Schoenbaum, S. *William Shakespeare—A Compact Documentary Life*. Oxford University Press, 1977.

Internet

Mr. William Shakespeare and the Internet: A list of the best Web sites on the great playwright and poet. Perfect for school—includes analysis, glossaries, even tests to check knowledge. Notice the virtual tours of the Globe Theatre.
http://www.palomar.edu/Library/SHAKE.HTM

Tapes

Ball, Patrick and Daniel Drasin. *Celtic Harp, Volume Two*. (Haunting and lyrical folk music of the British Isles as played on the celtic harp), Fortuna Records, Novato, California, 1983.

The following tapes are available through the Tutor Guild, Oregon Shakespeare Festival, 15. S. Pioneer, Ashland, Oregon, 97520:

Actors of the Oregon Shakespeare Festival. *Selected Sonnets of William Shakespeare*. Oregon Shakespeare Festival, Ashland, Oregon, 1990.

Kennedy, Judith. *Popular Dances of the Renaissance, Dance Music with Instructions*. Oregon Shakespeare Festival, 1985.

Musicians of the Oregon Shakespeare Festival, 1990 Season. *In Midst of Woods*. Recorded Freeman Studios, Ashland, Oregon, 1990.

Musicians of the Oregon Shakespeare Festival, Terra Nova Consort. *Somewhat Musing*. Freeman Studios, Ashland, Oregon.

Videos, Movies

A Man for All Seasons, with Orson Welles.

Lady Jane. Paramount Studios, 1986. This film, while romanticized, gives a fairly accurate picture of the times during the reign of Edward VI and the weeks immediately following his death when Lady Jane Gray came to the throne of England for nine short days.

Richard III, with Sir Lawrence Olivier.

Romeo and Juliet, produced by Zefferelli, 1968. One film treatment of the play in which teenagers play the roles, rather than older actors and actresses. Outstanding.

West Side Story, starring Natalie Wood as Maria in a musical with modern urban setting, composed by Leonard Bernstein and based on plot of *Romeo and Juliet*.

Multimedia CD-ROM

Romeo and Juliet: Center Stage. Sunburst Communications. This is a student production of the play followed by interviews, discussions, and explanations supplied by the student actors themselves. Highly recommended.

Shakespeare's Life and Times. Intellimation. This puts Shakespeare's work into context, containing text and concordances for 20 plays, over 200 color pictures of Renaissance life and art, and video clips of dance and music.

Answer Key

Quiz Time: Act I, page 10
1. Accept all appropriate responses.
2. the chorus
3. Verona, Italy
4. the Capulets and the Montagues
5. to woo her, win her heart
6. Both talk alike, often of silly things.
7. Accept appropriate responses which describe the ball and how they meet and react to each other.
8. He thinks of only her. His speech becomes poetry.
9. Tybalt wants to kill Romeo, but Capulet tells him to calm down and leave Romeo alone.
10. Accept all appropriate responses.

Quiz Time: Act II, page 17
1. Accept all appropriate responses.
2. He falls in love at first sight, and his love inspires poetry.
3. No. She is asking, "Why are you the son of my family's enemy, why is your name Romeo?"
4. Because she falls in love at first sight, too, instead of playing hard to get.
5. They will kill Romeo.
6. Because the day before, Romeo had been in love with Rosaline. The friar hasn't been able to keep up with Romeo's loves.
7. Mercutio
8. to help Romeo and Juliet marry
9. They agree to meet in Friar Lawrence's cell, where he will marry them.
10. Accept all appropriate responses.

Observing the Oxymoron, page 18
loving hate: Act I, Scene 1
sweet sorrow: Act II, Scene 3
bitter sweeting: Act II, Scene 4
honorable villain: Act III, Scene 2
Sick health, heavy lightness, and brawling love are all in Act I, Scene 1

Quiz Time: Act III, page 22
1. Accept appropriate responses.
2. Tybalt
3. Tybalt calls Romeo a villain. Romeo says that Tybalt does not know him well enough to call him that.
4. because he will be dead
5. exile from Verona
6. She feels terrible that Tybalt, her favorite cousin, is dead, and worse that Romeo killed him.
7. Nurse
8. Her father has willed her to be married to County Paris.
9. marry County Paris, or he will kick her out
10. Accept appropriate responses.

Romeo and Juliet Word Search

```
Q F S H A K E S P E A R E B L L I O M L N W
W R T Y U S T R A T F O R D U P O N A V O N
E E E U I G D I O A A M O N T A G U E K B F
R E W O P H S U P Q S E N V M K I P M J N D
T L W M A N T U A W D O N C N J U L N H B Q
Y I A P L J Y V E D A M X B H Y K B H V W
U Z S R K K B Y E R F N U R S E T J V L C E
U A D I J L A T R T G D L G A L I L E O X R
I B E N V O L I O Y H J M S D G R H V N Z T
O E G C H M T R N U J U L A V F R G C D Y T
P T F E F N A C A P U L E T C S E F X O A U
L H G S D B Q E P F R I A R L A W R E N C E
K I H A Z V W E O I J E K A X A W D Z G S I
N I J Z X C M E R C U T I O Z A Q S A F D O
```

Quiz Time: Act IV, page 27
1. Accept appropriate responses.
2. marry Juliet
3. Friar Lawrence
4. help Juliet fake her own death
5. in a drug-induced sleep in the family crypt
6. Mantua
7. tells him she will obey him
8. She is already married; she doesn't love Paris.
9. Juliet, apparently dead
10. Accept appropriate responses.

Quiz Time: Act V, page 32
1. Accept appropriate responses.
2. Mantua
3. He believes Juliet will soon be there with him.
4. news that Juliet is dead
5. because he must attend Juliet's family
6. outside the crypt; they fight, Romeo kills Paris.
7. He thinks Juliet is dead.
8. sees there is no poison left in his vial, stabs herself with Romeo's knife
9. He tells him all about Romeo and Juliet's being married, the mix-up with the letter, etc.
10. Accept appropriate responses.

Objective Test and Essay, page 43
Matching
1. b   2. j   3. i   4. g   5. h   6. f   7. e   8. c
9. l   10. d   11. a   12. k
True or False:
1. F   4. T
2. F   5. T
3. T
Short Answer:
1. Nurse
2. Accept all appropriate responses, including the following: Their families hated each other; Friar Lawrence and Nurse interfered; The blood feud between the Montagues and Capulets resulted in killings for revenge.
3. He married Romeo and Juliet,

knowing their families would disapprove; he helps them hide what they have done; he goes along with the Capulets' plan for Juliet to marry Paris, although he knows she is already married.
4. Verona, Italy
5. because she wakes from her sleep to find Romeo dead, and there is no poison left in his vial

Essay: Accept appropriate and well-thought-out responses.

Response, Page 44
Act I
1. said by the chorus in the Prologue
2. Capulet tells Paris to court Juliet.
3. Romeo says this about Juliet when he falls in love with her.
4. Juliet complains that she has fallen for her family's enemy.

Act II
1. Romeo is looking up at Juliet's window.
2. Juliet wonders why Romeo has to be the son of her family's enemy.
3. Romeo and Juliet part, planning to marry the next day.
4. Nurse tells Juliet to go quickly to Friar Lawrence' cell to marry Romeo.

Act III
1. Tybalt tries to provoke Romeo into a fight.
2. Romeo is exiled for killing Tybalt.
3. Juliet is thinking of marrying Romeo, telling how she loves him.
4. Juliet goes to the Friar to ask for help.

Act IV
1. Friar Lawrence has been told that Juliet will marry Paris Thursday, and he does not tell anyone she is already married.
2. Friar Lawrence tells Juliet he has something which will make her sleep as though dead.
3. Juliet drinks the potion the friar has given her.
4. Friar Lawrence, having still not told that Juliet is already married, comes to the house to find that everyone thinks her dead.

Act V
1. Romeo asks for word about Juliet from the friar, telling him what to do.
2. Friar John was supposed to take a message to Juliet from Friar Lawrence but did not.
3. Romeo plans to kill himself in Juliet's tomb.
4. Juliet wakens to find Romeo dead and no poison left in his vial.